PODCAST FORMULA

Grow Your Business By Having Conversations

BY ROBERT PLANK

Negative

Podcast Formula:

Grow Your Business By Having Conversations

By Robert Plank

© 2020 by Double Agent Marketing LLC, 408-277-0904

Introduction

With all the podcasts out there, how the heck do you stand out and how do you create something different? How do you make a podcast show that is fun for you, that keeps you motivated, that keeps you excited, but is also something that helps and grows your business and as something that can make you money or get you attention or get people interested in the specific cause that you want them to get interested in?

Whether you're a new or existing podcaster, there are so many podcasts out there and it almost feels like a handful of podcasts get all the attention and so many other podcasts are dead, none updated. They're not very great, but there's always that joke that you don't have anything to do. You have too much free time. It's time to start YOUR podcast. There are so many podcasts out there, but how will you get those raving fans that you always hear about? How will you get people to be excited about your next episode, to post a good review, to write in or email in, and give you ideas or tell you how much they love your show.

Podcast Must make Money.

- "White psychosis"

- Black people with it
"Vicarious White psychosis"
Sufferers.

2

Chapter 1: I Was Jealous!

Unique — You really are.

I was jealous about some of these shows or some of these people that seem to get all of the attention on the internet and I was confused about a million different things. I had no idea what I needed to say. I did not know what people wanted, and I saw some of these successful podcast shows with hundreds or sometimes thousands of episodes and I had no idea how I could create five or six episodes, let alone hundreds of episodes. I felt like it would be too much work, too much of an uphill climb, too much of a struggle to create the content that I knew I would need in order to talk about all the different subjects and to keep other people entertained, to keep me entertained. I knew that I would run out of things to say quickly and I knew that I would run out of people who would listen.

What's the Point?

What is the point of you recording a podcast, say every week, for 20, 30, 60 minutes including preparation, if only five people are listening to you? If the podcast does not make money, if the podcast does not excite you? Let's talk about some of those things. Let's talk about how to grow your podcast using website and using social media in order to get people tuning in to get people eager to what you have to say and to have a steady influx of new people who find out about you and find out about your show and are attracted to you because of the different topics that you talk about, but also stay because of the uniqueness that makes you fun and exciting.

White women intend to start talking about 'their' 'black' 'heritage' to get the 'Reparations' 'Money'. Stupid White Bitch.

Chapter 2: Tell Me If This Sounds Familiar...

I'm Robert Plank from podcastcrusher.com and tell me if this sounds familiar. You heard that you needed to write articles. You saw other people out there with so many blog posts. Maybe they even posted on a blog multiple times a day.

You went to some influencers Instagram page and you saw all the images they had posted, you went to someone else's YouTube channel and you saw that they posted something new at least every week.

Doesn't that seem discouraging? Doesn't it seem like you have no idea where to begin? Should you look at the front page of the news? Should you check out other people's websites and rip off their ideas or probably not?

I wanted a podcast. I wanted to have an easy way to communicate with my followers. I wanted to get new followers. That way they would buy my books, they would go to my websites, they would buy my courses, they would open my emails, but I had no idea where to begin. I was extremely confused. I even tried live streaming and I kept hearing this advice that, "Maybe you're just not posting enough content." I thought, "I'm posting content almost every day, all day."

I heard, "You need to look into this new social media platform or that new social media platform." And I thought, "I have already run out of time during the day and I'm not sure that posting to get five people to listen and posting some more to get five more people to listen is a sustainable business model."

Social Media

But just like you, I needed enough ideas for content and I needed some attention. And if you are looking to do things the hard way, if you want to spend all day, every day agonizing about every single word and sentence and video that you post online, then this is not a good solution for you. But this is a good solution for you if you want to be a podcaster in whatever niche, if this is a podcast that promotes your business but talks about lots of fun subjects. If you are looking for the easy way to get new people to discover you, then I have a specific plan that you can begin using to grow your podcast.

Chapter 3: I Was Working My Tail Off...

I was working my tail off writing blog posts, sending emails, looking into social media until it finally made sense. I needed to interview people for my podcast. It made sense because I noticed this is what everyone else in the world had been doing. Other podcasters would start a show, talk about topic after topic, but eventually they would run out of material and one of two things would happen. Either the podcasts would slow down and eventually die into nothingness or they pivoted into bringing other guests on their show who had fresh perspectives or who could talk about new topics that that podcast host did not specifically know about. This is what the talk shows do on TV.

I knew I could talk about internet marketing, WordPress, podcasting, publishing a book, but that was about it. If you think about your own skill set and about the things that you could record on a YouTube video or publish on a podcast, you are only knowledgeable about a handful of topics.

It was also interesting to have people on my show who were way out in left field. I had a guest who would interview an app creator after app creator on the Apple and Android web store. His name was Steve Young and had a show called App Masters.

How depressing ? !

I had a guest on name, Rob Lowe, who ran a nonprofit and he ran his own podcast where all the guests were people who also ran nonprofits. Now, think about what that does. It makes him appear as the thought leader because he has all

Thought Police.

these other nonprofit managing experts around him, but it also allows people that are in nonprofits that are outside of his expertise in other niches, in other countries, who have different takes than he does. And maybe they're even in the same niche, but they go about things a different way, or maybe they focus on a deep dive on one specific aspect of a nonprofit such as the accounting aspect of nonprofit or getting donors or running events. He could specifically get deep into a subtopic where he might not even feel like researching or talking about that sub topic. And above all, he could network. If there was something that his nonprofit specifically or his nonprofit expertise could help someone else or vice versa, now he found someone else.

Chapter 4: They Want Publicity!

These guests on all the other podcasts, they want publicity and the host of that podcast wants content and they want traffic.

When I began having guests on my podcast for interviews, I could then follow up. I could say, "It was great having you on my show. Now can you post about your appearance on social media? I've posted this quick clip on YouTube, can you link to that? Can you link to the podcast page itself?"

When I would have these guests such as Steve Young or Rob Lowe on my podcast, we posted that online. Now this person shows up in Google search results. I could post about the episode and then tag that person on social media. In the previous scenario, they might get annoyed or thinking I was spamming them.

Now, when I tag that person, it's a welcome happening. It's a welcome thing to do because they were on my show. I'm helping to promote their appearance on my show.

Think about what you could do. Think about the authors that you know that you could network with. Think about the books you've read, the software you use, the other influencers, the bloggers, the other podcasters that you can begin reaching out to and maybe you could reach out to some of the long shots, potential podcast guests that you might not get, but who knows if they reply. Maybe you can go for the sure thing, podcast guests. Maybe you can find a friend of yours that you are in a similar business with who recently put out a book.

Maybe you have an in with them. Maybe there're someone who's get-able. Maybe you can find a book on Amazon and see the book is only selling somewhat.

Contact that author and have them on your show. That way they'll be excited to sell more copies of your book.

If you're stuck about the content or the topics or the keeping going with your podcasts, consider podcast interviews. It takes so much of the pressure off of you. And you might be thinking, "How the heck do I do that?" It seems like an easy thing to understand. Podcasts eventually go to this interview format. I know that it probably is a good idea for me to have someone on my podcast. That way I can just ask them a few questions and they can provide the content for me, but what is there to know?

Chapter 5: It Starts With Their Bio

Anyone who has ever appeared on a podcast or wants to, has a quick bio. And if you want someone on your podcast, ask them for your bio. If they don't have a bio or they can't create a bio, you don't want them on your show anyway because they don't have anything to say. It starts with a bio and if you see their bio, if you like what it is that they have to say, if you think that they would be a good fit for your show. Now a good fit does not mean that they know exactly everything you do. It just means that they might have something that the listeners who know about your existing content might then want to know about something else.

I had a guest named Elena Herdieckerhoff, who is an expert in getting 1 million views to a TEDx talk. I can teach about a podcast, a book and a website, but I know nothing about getting on a TEDx talk, but if you think about it, if someone is listening to my show about a book, a podcast, a website, they want traffic, they want to get more attention to their business.

What better way to get attention to your business by speaking in front of a group of people and having this huge organization called TED promote you on their high-traffic YouTube channel and have a place where you can point people to and show them that you're an expert because you gave a TEDx talk. And that example, that TEDx experts is someone that my existing listeners would want to hear about, but that's also a topic where I myself might not know about that is a compatible topic.

Let's say that TEDx expert sent me her bio or I asked for it. I'll look at the bio and I would say, "Great, I would like to have you on my show." The next step is to have them schedule an appointment. We use a tool called Calendly, where we can set up office hours where we are available to meet for a podcast recording. They pick and choose the time spot that they would like. They show up. Then we knock out the recording.

Chapter 6: The ONLY Difficulty with Podcast Interviews

I ask this guest about themselves, what they're working on, about their business, about their struggles, about their emotional moments and ahas. And what's great about this is it puts all the pressure on that person. It makes it where you only have to ask a quick question and it's their job to pontificate for five to 10 minutes about that answer. You might be a little bit nervous about having guests on your show, but you are not the first show this person has probably been a guest on and you are certainly not the first person this guest has had a conversation with. They are guaranteed to be more nervous than you are to have them on your show because they're coming to your home turf.

The only difficulty is to figure out the back and forth, figuring out the rhythm that you have with a person because some podcast guests answer in 32nd bits, some podcast guests answer in five-minute responses. And if you can get a feeling on am I speaking with a fast or a slow talker or short-answer person or a long-answer person, then you get a better feel of meeting the person where they're at and don't try to make them conform to your speaking style. Meet in the middle, communicate, have a good conversation. This is by far the best way for you to get the word out about your business and about their cause and about their message. Because if you have to write every single thing you had to write, who knows how many hours would take. If you had to put everything on video and figuring out lighting and editing and music, podcasting is way easier because it's for the most part, audio only. You click a button, you go, you have someone on as an interview, you play a by ear. See where things happen.

You can and should record your podcast without a script or a plan. Over-planning adds more unnecessary work for you. It's more fun for someone listening if your show is not so polished. If they wanted something super polished, they could listen to talk radio, they could listen to Larry King. You are giving something different. You are delivering a real conversation that might sometimes be awkward, but for the most part goes off in unexpected directions where you work in your expertise, in your curiosity, and they bring their message to your audience.

What does this all have to do with you solving the growth problem of your podcast? What's this?

Chapter 7: Solve The "Growth" Problem

Many podcasters nerd out about the recording, about the equipment. They think that they need to record more content. The answer is that there needs to be more marketing. You can get more marketing of your podcast, if you go back and find a random old episode posted again on social media. Get guests on your show, or if you've had guests, contact them again, add them on Twitter, tag them on Facebook. Ask them to email their audience about their episode, their appearance on your show, and follow up with your guests. Ask them what else they need. Auto-post the links to your show or clips over time to social networks, and don't stop. Don't give up on your podcast. Always be on the hunt for a new guest.

You recently read a book or listen to someone else's podcast and you thought, "I'd like to have that guest on my show." Well, guess what? If someone's a guest on a podcast all ready, they're super duper more likely to be a guest on your show. Think about who you want to contact. Think about people you've met at events or offline or virtual events, or people that you would like to do business with or who would like to do business with you. Consider those people as guests on your podcast.

Dedicate just five minutes a day to growing your podcast. It's so easy to construct your world domination plans and go and record an episode and then months later you realize, "I have not touched my podcast in six months." Dedicate just five minutes a day. Would it not be better if you recorded a quick five-minute episode just catching your audience up on what you're doing or if you found an old clip from a two years ago episode and you said, "I was listening to this, this helped me. Here it is."

Mail your list about a past episode. Post on a social network. I would highly recommend you go to whatever online calendaring system you have such as Google Calendar, and post a recurring reminder every week or every couple of weeks to just devote five minutes a day. Or even better, find a friend, a buddy to every now and then nag you about your podcast and ask, "Have you put just five minutes a day into growing and keeping your podcast alive?" Because getting the word out about your podcast is more important than the words you speak on your podcast.

Conclusion

What's the point of having the best microphone, the best equipment, the best words, if you only have five listeners? Well, it's time for you to find more listeners for your podcast. That means contacting guests for interviews, posting more on social media, going back and remarketing your old episodes. It's not just about what you want to do with your podcast and get out of your own head.

It's easy to let your nervousness stop you from overthinking things, but as soon as you stop thinking about yourself and start thinking about where are people stuck when it comes to making money, when it comes to developing job skills, when it comes to getting themselves on a TEDx stage or marketing their nonprofit or getting an app created. Think about the problems that are out there. Find the experts that can help solve those problems. Get them on your show to have that mutually beneficial exchange where you get content, you get the name recognition of this guest, and they get the additional traffic that they now have because you have introduced your audience to them. Follow up again and use their network to grow your show. In this case, everyone wins. Think more about the people with your podcast, guests and your audience, and not so much as the things such as your equipment and all those geeky, techie details.

I'm Robert Plank from PodcastCrusher.com. Grow your podcast using a website and social media.

Resources

- PodcastCrusher.com: setup your podcast

- BookFormula.com: write a self-published book

- IncomeMachine.com: setup your online funnel

- MarketerOfTheDay.com: Robert Plank's podcast

- MarketerOfTheDay.com/378: Mobile App Marketing: Get More Downloads from App Store Optimization, Cold Emails to App Store Managers, and the Pay-to-Free Method with Steve Young

- MarketerOfTheDay.com/456: How to Become a TEDx Stage Speaker and Get Over 1 Million Views with Elena Herdieckerhoff

- MarketerOfTheDay.com/666: Focus, Leverage, and Value: Build Your Customer Base and Champion a Cause with Naresh Vissa

Thurs 16 July 2020

RAVEMailteam@
charitycommissions.gov.UK

Charity Commission Strategy
2018 - 2023 — gov website
See

Close a charity
Close/wind up a charity
T Brown.
                    (lesbian)
1. Joanne Pinnington
Sent link with lesbian
partner + picking.
A Racist!

About the Author

Robert Plank is an online business coach who would like to help you manage your time, get your life back, and simplify your daily activities.

Using systems, checklists, and templates, you can write a book within an hour and become a published author in 12 hours. You can setup a membership site in one day, create a blog or podcast in 5 minutes or less, and so much more.

- Book: PodcastFormulaBook.com

- Podcast: MarketerOfTheDay.com

Thursday 16 July 2020

Protector

Disclosure 4

Public Concern at
Work —
www. ~~pad~~ ~~pcg~~
PCaw.co.uk
at list the Report is
in to (SFO)

Leave a Quick Review

If you enjoyed (or hated) this book, want to give feedback or tell others what you thought of it, please me your honest opinion at:

PodcastFormulaBook.com/amazon

I look forward to hearing your thoughts.

" SFO Thursday, 16 July 2020
Confirmation 9.48am
ID: Wa 054 "

Report Regarding Lambeth
Council Corrupt in
Conspiracy, Regime Change
Planning or Regeneration
Not Mentioned "
Copy Communicate to me
email arc

23

CES

Thursday 18 J   £14·95

David Lloyd George

DVD

Greek Peter — Rent boy
(documentary)   £6·95

DVD

Printed in Great Britain
by Amazon